I0486702

Into The SMM Realm

Unleashing the Power of Social Media Marketing for Your Business' Success

By

Filcar Faunillan

Table of Contents

INTRODUCTION

I want to thank you and congratulate you for downloading the book, *"Into the SMM Realm: Unleashing the Power of Social Media Marketing for Your Business' Success"*.

Do you want to promote your business effectively, easily, and cheaply? Are you ready to take your business into what is in and trendy? If so, then social media marketing is the kind of business marketing strategy that you should take into consideration, and later on, into action.

Social media marketing is taking your business into the world of social networking sites and creating good noise of your business to a wide range of market. With millions and billions of people in different social networking sites, you will know that you are actually telling a huge audience about your business. And among all the billions and millions of these people, you can be sure that a lot of them could be interested with what you are offering, that is, if your strategy has been implemented well.

This kind of marketing is cheap and easy to do if you just learn the basics on how to do it. In this book you will learn what social media marketing is all about, how it works, why it is best for your business' growth, and how to manage it especially when it gets out of control.

Social media marketing is a new venture that your business should take, whether it is small or big, local or global. This is where you can sum up advertising and marketing under cheap cost. So, learn the basics of social media marketing and apply them for the betterment of your business.

Thanks again for downloading this book, I hope you enjoy it!

Chapter 1 - Welcome To The World Of Social

Media Marketing

If you have never heard of Facebook, Twitter, Instagram, or any other social networking site, perhaps you have been living under a rock. Almost everyone — people of different ages, races, and internet connection speed, have used the internet at one point or so in their lives. Perhaps you have used it for emailing others, keeping in touch with your friends and relatives on the other side of the world, researching for projects and papers, or even just for leisure and entertainment such as watching movies or listening to music. This advancement in technology, though, is also now used for more profit-oriented schemes such as marketing and advertising products and services of big and small businesses. Putting these businesses in the social media is what we call Social Media Marketing.

A. What is Social Media Marketing?

Social Media Marketing is placing your business' identity and offers in different social media sites that promote high interaction among its users. These social media sites may include Facebook, Twitter, Instagram, YouTube, Google Plus, Tumblr, and many more. These are websites that have millions and billions of users from all around the world that could possibly become your customers. This is the kind of opportunity that people who want to put up new business or create better identities of their old business should grab.

This kind of marketing has been acknowledged by 92% of Hubspot's business respondents as an essential venue for the growth of their businesses. This huge population of businesses in the social networking sites may mean increased competition but if you do not dwell into it as well, you will be missing out on a lot of chances. Social Media Marketing is a must for any kind of business, whether it is a small one or a well-known business already.

B. Why Social Media Marketing?

The internet is more than just an avenue for chitchatting and entertainment. Its capacity to tap a huge chunk of the world's population at whatever time of the day is one of the key factors on why it is also a great way for introducing your product or service. More than just for mere conversations, business transactions may also be made over the internet and that is immediately spread around through the use of social networking sites. From this cause, these are the reasons why you should choose Social Media Marketing as one of your platforms in introducing, promoting, advertising, and selling your goods and services:

Reason #1: It is undeniably fast.

Technically, the internet connection speed would determine how fast you can reach an audience in the internet, but compared to any other telecommunication device such as mobile phones and telephones, the internet can tap many people all at once in just a few clicks and taps. So, if you intend to say something urgent, the internet could help you with that.

Reason #2: It reaches a huge population—Either Local or Global

Social media marketing can help you tap a huge audience whom you can sort out into your target markets. Whether you want to stay local or go global, social networking sites will help you connect with your purposed market.

Reason #3: It encourages interaction both between customers and customers as well as customers and sellers

Social networking sites encourage social and virtual interaction between their users. So, this is how you can hear feedback coming directly from your customers. More so, they can also promote your items and services by their own free will especially when they were satisfied by them. They can talk about your business all by themselves and the more people get into the topic, the more your business hypes up.

Reason #4: High possibility of your product or service getting viral — exposure and traffic

Your market can freely talk about your products and services and once your customers get to use or experience them, they can have their feedbacks as well. This way, your business can become the talk of the cyber town. You do not even have to pay your customers to advertise your product or service. If they like it, you can just encourage them to review your site or page and tada! Others would know how well you can deliver as a business. This is a cheap way of promoting and advertising the business.

Reason #5: It is Remarkably Cheap

If you want to save up some money for business advertising and marketing, social media marketing is a sure way to go. With only a little investment — a smart phone, laptop, or personal computer, a strong internet connection, and good online interpersonal skills — you can already manage to run your business in the social networking sites available. Unlike other strategies of advertising the business — TV ads, Radio ads, newspaper ads, and others — the use of the internet is much cheaper.

Also, if you have a business in the cyber world, you do not always have to put up a store. There are small businesses in retail that can run even without a specific location of a store. You can go home-based and still earn even through social media marketing. Social media marketing allows you to save up some money that you would have spent on having your business known or building a store for it. Thanks to this way of marketing, you can already earn without investing so much money.

So, flip over and continue learning about how you can achieve and experience the benefits of Social Media Marketing for your own business.

C. Into Becoming a Social Business

Social Media Marketing is Social for a reason. This is the kind of marketing wherein you get a huge and a variety of participation from a wide range of people involved in your business — your stakeholders, customers, and employees. The purpose of building a social business lies on the creation of collaborative and innovative objectives as well as clear and meaningful engagements from the people involved in the business.

But How Do You Create A Social Business?

1. Encourage Participation From Different Parties

The essential people in your business are your stakeholders, your employees, and your customers. You have to train your employees or the managers of your social media page to become sociable and professional online — in posting content and in interacting with the customers or interested people.

Customers are not always complainants and whiners. That is why there is no need to get frightened when they comment about your product or service. As long as their critiques are for the betterment of your business then do not disregard them entirely.

You have to keep an open mind in hearing feedbacks from your customers because the more that you are, the more you can encourage participation from them. This makes them feel that their opinions are valued by the business. Most especially when these opinions are addressed with courtesy or even with direct action.

2. Utilize Social Media Applications

Social applications and websites in smart phones or computers are the backbone of the implementation of social media marketing. These sites are important components in bringing altogether your customers with the same interest as you and who will be convinced to try and later on, use your product or service.

Some of these social applications and websites are the well-known Facebook, Twitter, Instagram, Pinterest, Google Plus, and many more. Whichever platform you choose, you have to consider each of the tools and functions of these different websites and applications.

3. Be an Active Listener

People outside of your business may talk about your business. Some of their comments may seem neutral to you, some may be insulting, and some may be very flattering but whatever these comments may be, you have to be an active listener to all these talks.

Active listening is a skill that you need to have in managing a social business most especially that listening is a key component of communication. This means listening intently to understand and not just to hear or to know what is being said by the customers or audience of your business.

With active listening you may appropriately respond to the needs and desires of your customers most especially when their opinions are for the betterment and growth of your business.

4. Integrate What You Have Listened To

The step-up in valuing your customer's comments are listening to monitoring to active listening and then down to responding. The last part entails a crucial decision-making skill that will have to always be appropriate and timely.

Some comments and opinions may sound degrading at first but try to see their words in a more objective perspective and be very open about it. More so, integrate all the comments and see for yourself what most complaints are about so you can improve on them. You may also see the trending parts of your business that are loved by your customers. You may keep this or improve this to keep the loyalty of your customers.

There are many aspects of the different platforms in which you can measure how well your social business is going social.

You may make use of all these tools and measurements to create an integrated interpretation of the temperament of your customers on your product or service.

Chapter 2 - The Social Media Audience

When you jump into marketing via social media, you have to know that the market in this field also have their own identity which you have to familiarize in order to deliver exactly what they need or want from you. Knowing your social media audience would have to include questions like the following:

Question 1: What social media platforms does your target market belong to?
Question 2: What social networking sites and apps do my audience keep their accounts active?
Question 3: When are the members of my target market active in social media?
Question 4: What kind of content or post does my market want to see in social media?
Question 5: What kind of information does my market share in their social media accounts?
Question 6: What kind of social media device does my target market use?

A. The Behaviors of Social Media Users

Getting to know how the social media audience think and tick will give you an idea on how to put up your business in the internet. How they behave, what they need, what they want, and where they usually flock will tell you where to direct your business in the social media.

➢ **Birds of the same feather may usually flock together**

The social media audience will have their own choices of social networking sites and application which they would engage in. Based on size, Facebook is the most populated social media networking site, followed by Google Plus, YouTube, and Twitter. It is best to observe where your target market usually flock.

People who are more open to high levels of interaction would be active in Facebook or other sites that encourage chatting and sharing of information. Those who majorly prefer other kind of media like videos and pictures would usually be in YouTube or Instagram. So, if your products and services fit more in certain mediums, you might want to consider where your target market could be flocking.

- **Birds of the same feather have common schedules**

Observe when the social media accounts of your target market hype up with active users. It could be early in the morning when they hurry to check latest updates or late at night when they are relaxing. Whatever time of day that the members of your target market usually log in to their social media accounts should keep you alert. This is when you strike while the iron is hot... and active.

Knowing how many online users there are at a certain point of the day will keep your efforts focused and well invested. When you post an update when there are many active users, you will be assured that the information you have posted will be seen by a number of audience immediately—increasing its chances of going public and viral.

➢ **Your Audience May Also Be Everywhere**

An average internet user usually has 5 social media accounts, 2 of which he or she updates very occasionally. Multiple social networking site and application usage will give you an idea on which substitute sites you can put up your business in as well. It may sound a little creepy but you have to follow your target market or make sure that they get the information that you want to share to them. You have to have an active presence in the main and substitute social networking sites in which your target market usually spend their time and you have to make sure that you are all there together at the same time. This is how you get to them.

- **They will take their virtual lives into their own hands.**

Smartphones make it easier for the cyber people to check their social networking accounts at any time of the day, anywhere where there is a Wi-Fi connection. Applications for different social media site are not moving into mobile phone applications as well to suit the change of technology as well.

- **If you are putting up your business in the social media, you might as well keep up with moving your site to an application.**

You may tap social media networking sites in promoting your own business. You may use Facebook as an avenue for you to put up your business if you know that your target market is crowding in that social media. Putting that up in Facebook would mean your audience could check out your updates through

Facebook application as well. The same goes for other social networking sites with mobile applications.

- **Different Age Groups Have Different Social Media Motivations**

A lot of people of different ages engage in social media already and these different age groups have different reasons as to why they use social media networking sites and applications.

People of ages 16 to 24 are motivated by their fear of missing out on activities of their society and group of friends. Which is why they live in highly interactive and updated websites to keep track of the latest happenings and trends around them. They are also those who use the internet for information as well as they are those who are still in their studies.

Those who are of ages 25 to 34, are more into putting their work into their social media accounts. They are those who share posts regarding the details of their lives, network, and their work.

Those 35 to 44-year olds use social media to maintain or reconnect with old friends and promote and talk about their work.
Meanwhile, 45 to 64-year olds use the internet for networking and keeping in touch with friends and relatives whom they have not seen in a while already. Until then, the use of these social media networking sites becomes a habit that people learn to do.

B. Finding Your Target Audience

Now that you are already familiar with the kind of people that there are in the different aspects of the social media, perhaps you have already formulated an idea on which social networking site you can look for your target market. Finding your target market will be less of a tedious task with the information on their behavior and dynamics in the social media. Knowing how these people in the social media work will make them become more predictable in terms of location and social media networking site choice. Now, all you have to do is do the basics of spotting and keeping a community of your target market in social media.

- **Step 1: Define and Establish Your Target Market**

With the vision, mission, and goal of your business, you will have an idea on what kind of customers you are really looking for. Different social media networking sites users may have different characteristics that are reflected by their choice of active accounts. But even before you go and look for them, you have to know first what you are going to look for.

So, begin your search by defining your target market. Are they those who have high incomes? Are they the choosy type? Are they those who value quality over quantity or the other way around? Are they those who will also bite into whatever is trendy?

Whatever characteristics you are looking for in your target market, define them. State them. That way, you will get a clearer picture on where you can actually find these people in the social media.

- **Step 2: Do the Researching**

This is where you put in all the efforts of knowing where you can find your target market. You may test the waters by observing the people in different social mediums but you can also do the research on where exactly you can find the target market that you have already defined.

More so, if you have already chosen a platform to put your business in then it would be another duty for you to research on what your market wants. Social media promotes high interaction so it would not be hard for you to find out the buzz of your market. You can always take not of their shares, comments, posts, and feedbacks.

- **Step 3: Hop Into the Ride**

Social media is social for a reason. It involves free and therefore high interaction between users. So as the business owner, you can have the chance to talk directly to your customers. Issues and requests may be addressed immediately and easily through the kind of communication that the platforms offer.

Now that you have found your market, communicate with them. Keep a business-like yet friendly relationship with them. After all, you want to keep their loyalty to your brand. Keep yourself updated with the internet environment—both with the trends and your customers' demands and requests. Listen to them and continue engaging.

Chapter 3 - How To Begin And Win In Social

Media Marketing

A. Facebook

Facebook is one of the most commonly used social networking sites in the cyberspace. Its huge population of people of varied cultures and values whom you can connect with in order to entice them with your business.

You may start up your business in Facebook by creating its very own page with all the basic information that the customers need to know about it — the location, store hours, contact numbers, products, services. Basically, the customers need to know what the business is all about.

After you have created your page, start inviting your friends to like it. The very first people whom you can tell about your business will always be those people you know. However, you may also take a leap further and run a search in Facebook for people who could be interested in what you are offering. Tap these people and connect with them. Once you have spent some time reaching out to them, keep this communication burning. Do not lose this connection. Continue building the bridge.

More so, find a way to make your page unique — be it through your posts and promos. Make sure that the content of your page is exceptional and appealing to the customers.

And most of all, keep your account customer-friendly but stick to your business. Promote a sense of community even just within your page. Do not forget to listen to your customers feedbacks, after all, they are whom you are trying to win. However, also learn to how sift their comments. There will be those who will only want to make a noise but there will be comments that are critical enough. Listen to comments that will definitely make your business become better.

B. Google+

Google+ offers you more than 150 million active users whom you can convince to buy your products or services. It is under the umbrella of the very well-known website, Google.

Google plus can serve you with authorship, relationship marketing, and traffic creation.

Putting up your business in Google+ could help position it in the search results in Google. So, when people search for products similar to what you offer, you will be one of the first few results to be seen by the researchers. Google+ also offers Google Hangout which can help you connect and build relationships with your customers. Having your Google Plus profile will simply create little noise about your business. The more unique your content is, the more it can catch attention. And that is the first thing that you want to grab off of your target customers.

C. Instagram

Visual marketing is trending as business people are starting to grab the chances on visual imagery's attractiveness to the masses. With around 90 Million active users, Instagram is definitely one of the on-hand efficient platforms that would help your business grow.

Big names such as Starbucks, MTV, Marc Jacobs, Nike, and even Red Bull have jumped into social media marketing in Instagram. However, even small brands can engage in this mobile application to further extend their customer coverage.

Begin gathering your audience by searching hashtags that are similar you're your product and start following accounts of the same interest. Invite your friends and acquaintances as well. Keep the activity of your own account coming and make sure your photos will win your audience's hearts.

Instagram will make it easy for you, as business person, to keep track of how well you are doing as a business. You can track the hashtags that you promote your customers to use when they post a photo of your product or while they are experiencing your service. The number of likes, comments, re-grammed posts, and overall reach can also be used as your measurement on how effective and efficient you are in using Instagram as your avenue to advertise and market your items and services.

Optimize this chance of winning your customers' attention by posting beautiful photos—you can do artistic presentations of your products and behind the scenes and the-making posts. Make sure that your pictures will be presentable. Post them when activity among your Instagram followers are active.

a. Pinterest

Like Instagram, Pinterest utilizes the attraction power of visual marketing. It makes use of photographs and links to promote products, services, and even advocacies.

In Pinterest, you may create boards to compile photos of your products. Make your titles of these boards catchy and appropriate for whatever it is you are selling.

Also, use keywords in your description of these products. Use tags to make your photos easier to find. The easier they are to find, the more it can become viral and known by the interested public. More so, you can use a "Pinterest for Business" to measure how your account and business is doing in Pinterest.

b. Twitter

With more than 232 Million active users every month, Twitter is a good place to

tell the world about your business—even just in 140 characters.
But how exactly can you use Twitter for social media marketing?

Twitter offers different mediums on which you can post your announcements or advertisements. You can use photos, video clips, link other videos, and even just plain text for social media marketing in this site.

Start off by putting up an account with a biography that briefly describes what your business is about. Then get your audience and customers by searching for tags that relate to your product and follow those who are interested in those topics or products.

You may also start following those who are influential in your field of business—journalists, bloggers, politicians, or even potential business partners. Keep them close in your network so you can have easy taps when you will need their expertise.

Then fill your account with tweets relating to your product. Tweet as if you are entertaining your audience. You do not have to flood your followers with tweets but you do have to make sure that you tweet, at least, regularly. Regular tweeting shows your followers that you are actually still there. It is a sign of an active and a healthy profile.

Once you get the hand of promoting your business through scrambling 140 characters, then you might want to know how well your marketing in Twitter is working. You can track your mentions and see what your followers (or even non-followers) say about you. Feel the temperature of your customers by listening to what they actually have to say about your product or service. Take their comments as a chance for your business to improve. However, you still have to keep in mind on whether or not taking their suggestions would still be in line with your business' mission, vision, and goal.

Make use of Twitter analytics and check out what your best days to tweet are and what your followers favor of your tweets, content-wise. Take note of these points so you will know what parts of your business you could further improve.

c. Tumblr

You have to begin by making your own account and blog. But to your advantage, if you are a business person with a number of small businesses then you can just add a blog on the same primary account that you have made. Go to tumblr.com or install the application on your smartphone and get started with signing up.

Before you add up the basic information about your business, you have to think of a domain name for your blog. This name has to be legit and formal so people would know that your business is a real one and not some spamming dealers. Choose your domain name wisely because it would reflect your business' image. After that, provide basic information regarding your business.

The most challenging part in Tumblr is gaining followers. Some users have had their blogs for years and still have less than a hundred followers but if you are an active blog who invests on promoting your blog then it is highly possible that you can earn a thousand followers in just a month or two.

You can start of by following blogs whom you consider to be client prospects. Once they see that you have followed them, they may consider checking your blog out and once they see that you have presented well your posts and information, chances are they will follow you back. Then you get your first-hand possible customers. You may also tap on famous Tumblr users to include you in their promos so their followers would get to hear about your business. If this interests them then most likely, they would also follow your blog. Most of all, do not forget about using the hashtags. Some Tumblr users out there may want to follow your blog but they just have not heard about it yet. So by putting relevant tags on your posts, they will be able to find them just by searching them out in Tumblr.

Now that you have followers, your posts and updates about your business will now have their audience. Use the different mediums and features of Tumblr to your advantage when you announce new items, promos, sales, and other events of your business and update every once in a while.

Tumblr is good for businesses that need to post more content as it is a blog that can be utilized for businesses as well. Tumblr is easy to use and is joined by many people from different places of the world. These people may be your target market. Sifting through the interests of these people is made easy by Tumblr's suggested pages as well so it would be easier for you to find people who may be interested with what you have to offer.

Chapter 4 - An Easy Guide To Surviving Social

Media Marketing

The thing about Social Media Marketing is that it is very dynamic. Whatever is trending now may change in a while or whatever hits the masses may no longer leave a mark, which is why it is very important that you keep a close distance and alert eyes on the changing scenes and temperatures of the social media people and platforms.

Keeping yourself updated with these changes or even anticipating these changes and planning ahead will keep you one step ahead before all the other businesses in the same line as yours. More so, knowing how your competitors are working will tell you how well you are working as well or if you are really working that well.

To venture into the field of Social Media Marketing will be an effective choice. Still, the guarantee lies on how you handle your business in the world of fast-changing temperaments and trends. You must hold your horses and be ready to hit the road whenever you have to.

These are the following tips on how you could keep your business in the Social

Media going at par or even better than everyone else:

- **Learn the Basic Threes: Observe, Input, Measure**

You have to learn how your customers behave, what they want, what they need, and how much they are willing to pay and do just to get their desires and needs.

Observing your market would be the first thing that you have to consider before you even position your business in the social media. Knowing your potential customers could give you an idea on how you could offer them your products and services. Perhaps they have certain values that you also have to consider or beliefs that you could work on in convincing them to get enticed with your business.

Take in what you have observed and apply little inputs on what you could put up for these observations. Perhaps you can match up your advertising mediums by knowing that your audience are people who respond more favorably to visual stimuli. If they do then you may use photos and videos in your product placement.

Then, once your business is already out there in the internet, you may already make use of the analytics of the different platforms. Different sites have different measurements on how much activity your age is making —whether you know it through tags, mentions, number of followers, and reposts. These are different guides for you in knowing how well you are doing in the social media marketing industry.

- **Keep Yourself Updated**

One of the important things that you need to know about the cyber space is that a lot of information in there could get viral in just a matter of seconds. There are changes in the social media networking sites as well as your social media marketer competitors that could affect your business in one way or another.

It is important that you also keep track of the changes in the platforms. Take note of what is trendy because that will keep your customers holding on to your business. If changes may occur in other competitors, watch out if these changes could impact your business.

The cyber world is a dynamic place to position your business in, especially when you compare the positioning to more traditional mediums such as print ads and even direct selling. Those strategies differ in terms of pacing. Still, it is key to keep yourself updated with whatever happening around you. Chances are, there could also be new opportunities for you to improve your business as well.

➢ **Utilize Emotional Appeal on Your Customers**

Whatever choice of platform you may decide on and whatever mode of content postings you would choose, it would be best for your business to win hearts of your target customers. If you hook on emotional aspects of promoting your business in the social media, you can develop better customer loyalty.

You may have noticed ads in YouTube that sell more feelings than just their products or services. Or you may have also observed photos that could never fail to portray a thousand words. These are winning posts that can elicit emotional bonds between the customers and your product or service.

Informing your customers about your product is a start-up for your business when you put in the social media. However, to keep your customers coming over and over, they must be able to feel a sense of connection with your product or services. Even in social media marketing, information and emotions should go together. There also has to be a sense of meeting between the mind and the heart of the customers.

Chapter 5 - Streamlining Your Social Media

Accounts via Hootsuite, Crowdbooster, and Grabinbox

Have you once thought of linking all your social media accounts so what you post on Twitter for example, will be posted simultaneously on Facebook too? As your business grows and you become too busy monitoring your sales, chances are, your social media marketing efforts might be put aside. Well, streamlining is possible as Facebook offers such linkage. However, having all social media accounts all in one place and getting all updates at the same time is possible so you don't need to switch from one to another allowing you to save time and is very cost-effective. Here are some of these tools that makes your updating easier and faster:

a. Hootsuite

One of the most popular social media tools, Hootsuite enables you to manage all your accounts be it Twitter, Facebook, Google+, Foursquare, Reddit, LinkedIn, and a lot more plus connect your WordPress site. Schedule unlimited posts straight from its dashboard ahead of time and get analytics so you know that all you SMM efforts are not being put to waste.

b. Crowdbooster

Know who are your influencers, what time your posts are most visible, which times should you post, and you can be sure you have your engagements straight with the aid of Crowdbooster. Insights are given per post so you get an idea on what to improve next.

c. Grabinbox

Unlike Hootsuite and Crowdbooster, Grabinbox is less popular yet another effective SMM tool and this is offered for free.

Chapter 6 - The Dos and Don'ts in Social Media Marketing

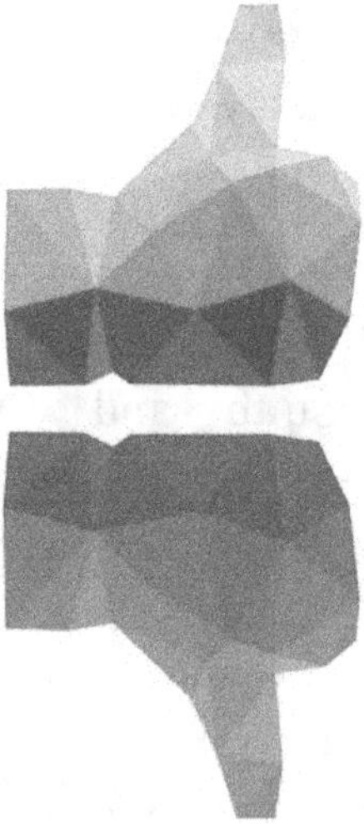

One of the things that you have to consider in facing a lot of audience in the social media is the fact that many of them could also be the judges of your posts and updates as a business page. It will take you a lot of effort to gain interested customers and only a single mistake to lose them. Which is why you have to be mindful with what you post in your business page.

a. Social Media Marketing Etiquette

A lot of things in the internet can get viral in just a few clicks. You are lucky if your business' good feedbacks will spread faster than fire in the cyber world. But remember that bad news can also spread as fast as any other news in the social media and stopping it in an instant may seem like a futile discourse. This kind of crisis will need a strong and firm management and in order to do that, there are a few things that you need to know about social media marketing etiquette.

➢ Do not ignore comments

You created a social media account for your business to expand its reach to a wider audience in the internet. Once you have gained interested customers, you might as well want to keep then in your list. A lot of your audience may criticize your product and services, and even in business, you have to know that you really cannot please everyone. Whatever comments your audience and customers may give you, as much as possible, answer them politely. Acknowledge their comments and answer truthfully and courteously no matter how mean or degrading their comments may be. Keep a cool head and a professional mannerism in handling comments of your audience.

- **Give credits when it's due**

If you intend to include quotations on your posts or use photos that are not yours, you might as well give credit to whoever said those words or took those pictures.

You may be issued with plagiarism and your business' reputation may be put at risk if you are not careful with giving credit when it is due.

➢ **Do not hijack threads or posts with self-promotion**

Yes you want to endorse your business and yes you want people to know about it but hijacking conversations just to promote your own business most especially when the thread does not even talk about what you are offering is a definite no-no. Improve your own content and page and avoid disrupting conversations that does not have anything to do with your business.

➢ **Check Your Grammar**

The social media world may be full of grammar Nazis and you have to remember that as a public account your posts may be seen by a lot of people. Your posts will be subjected to your audience's criticism and judgment. So if your posts contain wrong grammars, prepare for your audience's corrections.

Perhaps you have seen Instagram accounts who comment on different posts that does not have anything to do with their business. If you own the photo they commented on, how would you feel? Some of the people may only be irritated by that kind of promotion. So as much as possible, do not hijack other people's conversations and posts for the sake of endorsing your business.

- **Keep a Transparent and Honest Relationship With your Customers**

You may have beautified your photos, videos, or music to the maximum level that they do not entirely show the real product already. This is a big No-no in social media marketing. You are in the social media networking site to get closer to your customers easily so you could develop a strong customer-seller bond.

And that is definitely not bound to happen if deception rules over your business.

So keep in mind that beautifying your posts—photos and videos, does not mean you have to overdo the filter usage or exaggerate your editing skills because the customers need transparency for trust. And you will need their trust to keep them loyal to your brand.

- **Do Not Over-Hashtag Your Posts**

Tags seem will lead your customers to your product or service when they search for them in the engines. However, too much usage of hashtags especially those that are already irrelevant to your business will annoy the audience.

If you are a marketer who sells ready-to-wear clothes and includes #books in your hashtags, the tendency is that people who are supposed to be looking for books will find your photo or post. And remember that misleading them is a kind of deception that cannot ever win customers.

- **Do not post or tag photos of fans, customers, or employees without their request or permission**

Your goal is to get your brand known by refrain from forcing yourself into the accounts of your followers and friends. Avoid tagging them in pictures without their faces. There are people who do not want to be tagged with a picture of a bag (that is not even theirs!) or a blouse. If you want to update them with your items you may ask permission from them if you could tag them whenever you update your albums so they would know. If they do not request or give their permission, do not post or tag them in your photos. If you do, be prepared for a fallout of your customer crowd.

➢ **Do Not Post Content With Broken Links**

Some of the content of your pages or accounts may be of links to other websites. However, before you post anything, make sure that the link is not a 404 Error: Not Found destination. This will create a bad impression to your audience. Simple postings, no matter how simple they may be, will have to go checking, most especially that your account is open to your customers.

➢ **Do Not Spam Your Audience**

Even as a personal account you would not want your dashboard to be filled with the same content from the same user. Not only is it annoying to scroll down to see other people's post but it creates a disorganization in the profile of the person who has spammed as well.

The key in making your posts hit the audience is keeping them short and concise but witty and direct to the point.

No matter how many your posts are, if they do not catch the audience interest, they will only be ignored. Even in posting, quality will beat quantity.

- **First Name Basis With Your Customers**

One of the most effective tactics of marketing is making emotional bonds with your customers. As a marketer, you have to be aware of the power of using names. There were studies that have shown that employees in fast food chains and other cafes like it better when the customers address them with their first name.

Do not underestimate the power of simply calling the customers by their first names. It is not that you may sound creepy, unless you intend to creep him or her out really, but replying to comments by calling the customers with their first names will sound more friendly and approachable. And as a seller, that is something that you should make your audience and customers feel.

- **Slow Down With the All-Caps**

You probably know what all-caps sound like: screaming. To emphasize something, you may use all-caps but to overdo it looks like you are screaming to your audience. Slowdown in using all-caps, instead, make use of exclamation points to show excitement and thrill.

- **Match Your Content With The Right Network**

When you post something, keep in mind the people you are posting for and put yourself in their shoes. Do they like visual posts? Music? Clever lines? And match your content with them. When you do this, it would be easier for you to gain their attention. Most probably they will be more interested with what you have posted and will stay tuned for more updates in your business by becoming a loyal customer. Even in social media marketing, matches will work their way to better relationships—that is, customer and marketer.

- **Do Not Automate**

You may have noticed Twitter accounts or Instagram posts that automatically send Direct messages or use hashtags and automated followers. Yes, these may be tactics to use to gain the people's interest but invading their cyber lives without their permission is a big no-no that you should definitely avoid as a marketer.

Automated posts is a no-sweat and no-effort marketing—in other words, it is a slacker's way of marketing which is why, as much as possible, do not make use of this tactic. The abundance of these automated tools will make it tempting but the more you gain your followers and customers through hard work and real effort, the more emotional your relationship and bond becomes.

- **Update, update, and update**

Your social media accounts will not buzz when they do not even contain anything that is of date. Let us put it this way, perhaps you have posted a photo of the menu of your little food business but that was 5 years ago and now the prices have changed already. So when a customer searches for your products your un-updated menu is what he or she will find. When that customer orders from you and find out that your prices have gone higher, do you think he or she will be happy? No. So make sure that what you have in your pages reflect your business' current state. This goes out to all other content of your page. Whether it is the location, if you have one (or even more), if it is the ending of a promo, if it is a beginning of one — just about anything that is worth informing your customers.

So update, update, and update. Keep your audience informed of what is going in your business — what promos you are offering, what new products you have, and how they can experience your services. Update but do not overdo it. Limit your posts to at least three to five times daily. Then, at least your customers will know that you still exist. Good page activity means good business condition so entice your potential customers with it.

- **Humanize Your Page or Account**

Business may be business in stance but that should not take away the humanization of it. Humanizing your business or brand simply means: celebrating successes, acknowledging others (customers, employees, and others), responding to comments individually and with courtesy, and admittance of mistakes if there are any.

The more your audience feel as though your brand is humanized, the more they can relate to you. And the more they can relate to you, the more you can hold their loyalty as customers of your business. Business may mean business but to veer away from its stoic state and showing little humanization is a good way to establish an emotional relationship with the audience.

➢ **Enjoy Your Marketing and Your Market!**

Most of all, as you humanize your business and connect with your audience, all you have to do is be at ease but keep an eye on changes in the trends and in the social media marketing world.

Yes, you may post jokes relevant to your business and yes you may talk to your customers as well and hear from them just as long as you live within your limits as a marketer. Still, living within your boundaries as a marketer does not hinder you from enjoying your job and the company of your colleagues and customers. Be competitive but do not be too hard on your own business. Yes, diamonds need pressure but remember that too much will always be a dangerous thing to a business. So give your business and yourself some times to breathe and be prepared to face obstacles with a more open mind and quick and correct skills.

b. The Social Media Marketing Disasters — the bad, the ugly, and the beastly

Different brands—known or not—may have experienced one social media post that have gotten out of control in one way or another. These experiences may have damaged their businesses entirely, some may have gotten lessons out of the mistakes, and some may have turned the tables to turn their mistakes into their own favor.

The following are true stories of some big names of businesses that have experienced social media marketing crises. How they handled these crises may be a laughing stock for some but it cannot be denied that these are sources of lessons as well.

1. Red Cross

One of the mortifying things of being a member of the admin of a social media account of a business is posting on a wrong account. Gloria Huang was the person behind the mortifying rogue tweet of #gettingslizzered of Red Cross.

However, Red Cross handled this mistake pretty well by saying:

"We are an organization that deals with life-changing disasters and this wasn't one of them"

Even handling a bad mistake like this could get a witty comeback from the organization r business. If this crisis happens to you then you may also use a clever way to respond and handle the problem.

2. DKNY

Brandon Stanton is the outstanding photographer of the page Humans of New York, you may wonder how he has come into picture with DKNY but this is what happened:

Brandon was asked by a New York representative of DKNY to take 300 photos for $15,000 for DKNY. After some serious consideration and advises, Brandon turned the offer down. However, his photos were spotted in a DKNY shop in Bangkok, Thailand. And the problem was terribly apparent in this one. Brandon Stanton posted on Facebook a complaint on DKNY saying:

"I don't want any money. However, kindly SHARE this post if you think that DKNY must give the amount of $100,000 to the Bedford-Stuyvesant Brooklyn YMCA. This said donation will be of great help to deserving kids who would attend the summer camp".

Whatever happened behind the closed doors of DKNY is not entirely known. However, they eventually overcame this crisis by giving in to the outcry of Stanton. DKNY donated the said amount to the YMCA on behalf of Brandon Stanton.

Still, despite the quickness and appropriateness of DKNY's response, the mistake was really something that could have been prevented. It was definitely wrong for DKNY to take Stanton's photos without permission. Lucky for them they were able to manage the mistake well.

3. Burger King

Hacking is one of the many dangers of the internet and Burger King has become a victim of it. Burger King's Twitter account was hacked and its name was changed to McDonald's. The hacker started promoting McDonald's instead and by the time Burger King got a hold of the situation, the hacker already gained 30,000 new followers for the account... only under the wrong impression. Although the result of the crisis was a good one, hacking remains to be a danger to any business in the social media industry. So secure your passwords, do not disclose them to anybody, and stay tuned with your account as much as possible.

c. The Social Media Marketing Crisis

You may intend to post something that would promote your business but it came out as insensitive and insulting to some of your audience. You may want to crack a joke and connect with your customers but some of them find your joke disgracing some other people. Despite all of your good intentions or whatnots, there may be times when mistakes will slip through your account's posts. Perhaps it may take you one breath to realize that you have made a mistake. Then your post or the news about your business has spread like wildfire already. But as the owner, you know you just can't afford to sit there and watch your business burn down to ashes. Crisis management is the kind of business matter that you have to master whatever your business may be, but it holds a lot of utilization in the social media marketing. However, before you decide to manage it, you must first recognize that it really is a crisis:

- **Information Asymmetry**

When what your business knows is different from what your audience knows, that is when the information becomes asymmetrical. When this happens, problems may occur and misunderstandings may ruin the reputation of your business.

- **Slip From the Norm**

Your business may hold an identity already. People may have a constant chatter about your business whether it's good or bad, but when it slips off from what you intend your audience to know about your business that is when you should take up a red alert. Your business may uphold a certain brand that people identify of and veering away from this identity you thought you have embodied in your business can shake up your business.

- **Material Impact on Company**

If the chatter roaming around about your business is seriously ruining its reputation and you notice that your sales have really been affected then you know that you really have to make an immediate move already. As much as possible, identify the problems quickly so you may be able to respond immediately as well.

d. How to Deal With Social Media Marketing Crisis

Fight or flight are the two basic ways of facing danger. But when it comes to facing the dangers and threats on your business in the social media marketing aspect you have to keep a fight mantra that does not involve name-calling and cyber cat-fights. Fighting does not necessarily mean you have to argue with those who started off the crises, it only means that you have to face these problems with a professional stance no matter what. If you intend to take a flight, your business may also have unresolved issues that will clutter its reputation into bankruptcy.

So, take your mind with you when you fight against social media crises and do not allow emotions to rule over solving these issues because once they do, matters become more and more personal and more and more complicated.

By following the steps provided below you may already learn the basics of fighting against reputation-ruiners in the social media industry. Keep them in mind and follow them whenever your business is faced with internet issues.

Step 1: Acknowledge

If you made a mistake—say you have been quite insensitive and insulting—acknowledge your mistake. Admit that you made a wrong move. Your denial will only worsen the situation and madden people more and more.

Step 2: Apologize and Explain

Once you have acknowledge that you have made a mistake or that there was a misunderstanding between you and the public, do what is needed: apologize and explain. When you explain, be firm about it. Do not point fingers or blame others. Claim your mistake and be done with it.

Step 3: Create a Crisis FAQ (Frequently Asked Questions)

Your audience may always have to ask about the crisis and most of the time, people just ask the same questions over and over again. The best you can do is create a section for the crisis' Frequently Asked Questions and provide explanations and answers. You may place this section temporarily in your biography, or if the platform provides a specific page, then use it.

Step 4: Know When You Should Take it Offline

After you have politely and briefly explained your side of the story in a post or a comment, make sure you have given out all the details that your customers need to know. Once one pushes a reply of degrading you still, avoid making a third reply. Third replies are not explaining, they mean arguing. And if you have already explained your side clearly, there is no need to sweat it out.

Step 5: Chill Out

Keep in mind that no matter how below the belt some comments might hit, it is your responsibility as a public figure in the line of businesses—no matter what size or scope—to remain professional. It can not be refuted that there could be customers who might not be pleased with your product or service and they will ruin your name in the most degrading way that is possible. But take a few deep breaths before replying. And when you do, still, act according to your profession. Business is business.

Social Media Crises therefore entails four plans: Prevention, preparation, proper response, and recovery. With all these actions planned and executed in the most effective and efficient way as possible, you do not have to worry about losing your business to social media crises. These are the four essential basics in handling your business' reputation in the social media market where traffic and dynamics are in a run. You have to be quick and correct in dealing with problems like social media crisis or else your business can flip over and lose its good reputation quicker than you have established it.

CONCLUSION

Thank you again for downloading this book!

After leaning by heart all the information incorporated in this book, you have got to ask yourself the following questions again:

Do you want to promote your business effectively, easily, and cheaply? Are you ready to take your business into what is in and trendy?

If you agree to all of these questions then you may already begin venturing into social media marketing. With a wide set of audience whom you can tap, connect, and convince to become your customers, you are opening up your chances of growing your business more and more at a cheaper cost and greater revenues than all the other ways of advertising and marketing. This book has given you the information on how to begin, go through, and keep up with social media marketing. So, now, do not miss your chance of experiencing the benefits of social media marketing to your business' development. No matter how big or small your business is, social media marketing is surely a great way to help it become known and build its brand name to gain more and more satisfied customers.

Finally, if you enjoyed this book, then I'd like to ask you for a favor, would you be kind enough to leave a review for this book on Amazon? It'd be greatly appreciated!

Thank you and good luck!

www.ingramcontent.com/pod-product-compliance
Lightning Source LLC
Chambersburg PA
CBHW072308200526
45168CB00014B/895
* 9 7 8 1 5 1 7 6 2 4 1 7 0 *